*A gift for*

_____

*From*

_____

# Great Attitudes!

## 10 Choices for Success in Life

### Charles R. Swindoll

Designed by LeftCoast Design, Portland Oregon.

www.thomasnelson.com

www.jcountryman.com

ISBN: 1-4041-0302-3

Printed and bound in USA

# Contents

~

his may shock you, but I believe the single most significant decision I can make on a day-to-day basis is my choice of attitude. It is more important than my past, my education, my bankroll, my successes or failures, fame or pain, what other people think of me or say about me, my circumstances, or my position. Attitude keeps me going or cripples my progress. It alone fuels my fire or assaults my hope. When my attitudes are right, there's no barrier too high, no valley too deep, no dream too extreme, no challenge too great for me.

Let me pause right here and ask you about your attitude. How is it? Perhaps it's good right now, but what about tomorrow morning when you punch in on the time clock? Or what about by the end of the day tomorrow evening? How will your eight to ten hours have been? As you work shoulder to shoulder with people in your shop, in your office, or among the sales force where you are employed, or in the administrative pool, what kind of attitude will you have?

The dictionary on my desk defines *attitude* as "a manner of acting, feeling, or thinking that shows one's disposition . . . opinion, mental set." That means that how we think determines how we respond to others. My attitude is a direct reflection of what I think, which in turn affects how I respond to others!

In the little letter Paul wrote to the Christians in Philippi, he didn't mince words when it came to attitudes. Although a fairly peaceful and happy flock, the Philippians had a few personality skirmishes that could have derailed them and hindered their momentum. Knowing how counterproductive that would be, he came right to the point: their attitudes. "If therefore there is any encouragement in Christ, if there is any consolation of love, if there is any fellowship of the Spirit, if any affection and compassion, make my joy complete by being of the same mind, maintaining the same love, united in spirit, intent on one purpose" (Phil. 2:1–2).

What does all this mean? Well, let's go back and take a look. There *is* encouragement in the Person of Christ. There *is* love. There is also plenty of "fellowship of the Spirit" for the Christian to enjoy. Likewise, affection and compassion. Heaven is full and running over with these things even though earth is pretty barren at times. So Paul pleads for us to tap into that positive, encouraging storehouse. How? By "being of the same mind." He's telling us to take charge of our own minds; clearly a command. We Christians have the God-given ability to put our minds on those things that build up, strengthen, encourage, and help ourselves and others. "Do that!" commands the Lord.

As your friend, let me urge you to take charge of your mind and emotions today. Let your mind feast on nutritious food for a change. Refuse to grumble and criticize! Reject those alien thoughts that make you a petty, bitter person. Let your life yield a sweet, winsome melody that this old world needs so desperately. Yes, you can if you *will*.

⟶ Charles R. Swindoll

Attitude is a choice.

A good attitude is a good choice.

*Life is 10 percent what happens to you*
*and 90 percent how you respond to it.*

# OPTI

*Choose an Attitude of*

# MISM

*A Can-Do Attitude*

ccording to the theory of aerodynamics, repeatedly demonstrated through wind-tunnel experiments, the bumblebee is unable to fly. This is because the size, weight, and shape of his body in relation to the total wingspread make flying impossible. But the bumblebee never read the report. Being ignorant of these scientific truths he just goes ahead and flies anyway!

That reminds me of a fellow in the Bible named Caleb who had a can-do attitude. When you study his life in the book of Joshua, you see that he was positive—even though the majority of others around him weren't, he was.

They said, "We can't." He said, "We can."

They said, "We shouldn't." He said, "We must."

They said, "It's impossible." He said, "There is no such word with God."

Taking on Life with a Great Attitude

*Deposit the Positive*

~

These minds of ours are like bank vaults awaiting our deposits. If we regularly deposit positive, encouraging, and uplifting thoughts, what we withdraw will be the same. And the interest paid

**Refuse to let your situation determine your attitude.**

~

will be joy. The secret lies on our mind-set—on the things we fix our minds on.

~ Laugh Again

## The Greater Good

~

During his days as president, Thomas Jefferson and a group of companions were traveling across the country on horseback. They came to a river that had left its banks because of a recent downpour. The swollen river had washed the bridge away. Each rider was forced to ford the river on horseback, fighting for his life against the rapid currents. Each rider was threatened with the very real possibility of death, which caused a traveler who was not part of their group to step aside and watch. After several had plunged in and made it to the other side, the stranger asked President Jefferson if he would carry him across the river. The president agreed without hesitation. The man climbed on, and shortly thereafter the two of them made it safely to the other side. As the stranger slid off the back of the horse onto dry ground, one in the group asked him, "Tell me, why did you select the president to ask this favor?" The man was shocked, admitting he had no idea it was the president who had helped him. "All I know," he said, "is that on some of your faces was written the answer 'No,' and on some of them was the answer 'Yes.' His was a 'Yes' face."

~ The Grace Awakening

~

ision is the ability to see God's presence, to perceive God's power, to focus on God's plan in spite of the obstacles.

When you have vision it affects your attitude. Your attitude is optimistic rather than pessimistic. Your attitude stays positive rather than negative. Not foolishly positive, as though in fantasy, for you are reading God into your circumstances. So when a situation comes that cuts your feet out from under you, you don't throw up your arms and panic. You don't give up. Instead, you say, "Lord, this is Your moment. This is where You take charge."

What's the secret of a great attitude?

Choice.

## The Right Attitude

~

When I'm able, by faith, to sense God's hand in my situation, my attitude will be right. I don't begin the day gritting my teeth, asking, "Why do I have to stay in this situation?" Instead, I believe that He made me the way I am and put me where I am to do what He has planned for me to do. I don't wait for my situation to change before I put my heart into my work. I suggest you give that a try. It's called "blooming where you are planted." There's nothing like an attitude of gratitude to free us up.

~ Joseph: A Man of Integrity & Forgiveness

## *Good News or Bad?*

~

Twelve men went in to spy out the land and came back with a report. (Joshua 13 and 14)

Ten of the men could only talk about how big the giants were. "Do you realize those guys are big?" they asked. Caleb's response? "Do you know how big God is? Human giants are zip compared to a universal-size God. It isn't about the enemies. God said He would give us the land. So why are we standing here with our faces hanging out worried about a few enemies? Let's get an attitude of fortitude and take 'em on'!"

Have you ever been in a crowd when bad news starts to spread? Little negative attitudes crop up and before you know it you are overcome with a negative spirit? Negativism always gets a nod over a positive spirit. That's why the evening news is full of it. They're not going to tell you it's almost sunny, they'll tell you it's partly cloudy.

They're not going to tell you what great things are happening over there in Orlando. They'll tell you about a mudslide in Malibu. Why? Because that is what gets your attention. Unless, of course, you're a person like Caleb who refused to entertain a negative attitude.

Have you ever had the courage to stand against that attitude? That's what Caleb did. The crowd was focused on the giants. Caleb was focused on God. It's not about us. It's about God.

What's the secret of a great attitude like that? Choice. You can choose to be a drag and a burden, or an inspiration and encouragement. How? By centering God in the very core of your being. Put Him right in the heart of your day. Start with Him, stay with Him. Believe His word. Trust Him.

∼ Taking on Life with a Great Attitude

Acceptance is taking
from God's hand absolutely
anything He gives, looking
into His face in trust
and thanksgiving.

~

*The Pursuit of Happiness*

~

he pursuit of happiness is a matter of choice
. . . it is a positive attitude we choose to express.
It is not a gift delivered to our door each morning,
nor does it come through the window. And it is certain
that our circumstances are not the things that make us
joyful. If we wait for them to get just right, we will never
laugh again.

~ *Laugh Again*

*An Optimistic Outlook*

〜

*I*n order for old defeating thoughts to be invaded, conquered, and replaced by new, victorious ones, a process of reconstruction must transpire. The best place I know to begin this process of mental cleansing is with the all-important discipline of memorizing Scripture. I realize it doesn't sound very sophisticated or intellectual, but God's Book is full of powerful ammunition! And dislodging negative and demoralizing thoughts requires aggressive action. And God's victorious promises are a good place to start. For example:

➢ *I can do all things through Him who strengthens me.*
(Phil. 4:13)

➢ *Those who wait for the Lord will gain new strength; they will mount up with wings like eagles, they will run and not get tired, they will walk and not become weary.*
(Isa. 40:31)

➤ *Do not fear, for I am with you; do not anxiously look about you, for I am your God. I will strengthen you, surely I will help you. . . .*
(Isa. 4:10)

➤ *These things I have spoken to you, so that in Me you may have peace. In the world you have tribulation, but take courage; I have overcome the world.*
(John 16:33)

~ Living Above the Level of Mediocrity

People who inspire others
are those who see invisible
bridges at the end of
dead-end streets.

~

*A Positive Perspective*

~

One of the greatest benefits to be gleaned from the Bible is perspective. When we get discouraged, we temporarily lose our perspective. Little things become mammoth. A slight irritation, such as a pebble in a shoe, seems huge. Motivation is drained away and, worst of all, hope departs.

God's Word is tailor-made for gray-slush days. It sends a beam of light through the fog. It signals safety when we fear we'll never make it through. Such big-picture perspective gives us a hope transplant, and within a brief period of time, we have escaped the bleak and boring and are soaring.

"Whatever was written . . . was written for our instruction, that through . . . the encouragement of the Scriptures we might have hope" (Romans 15:4).

~ Living Above the Level of Mediocrity

*Persistent Optimism*

~

All this talk about optimistic attitudes reminds me of a story involving some American soldiers during the Korean War. As was common among the GIs, they had rented a house and hired a local boy to do their housekeeping and cooking.

This little Korean fellow they hired had an unbelievably positive attitude—he was always smiling. So they played one trick after another on him.

They nailed his shoes to the floor. He'd get up in the morning, pull those nails out with pliers, slip on the shoes, and maintain his excellent spirit.

They put grease on the stove handles, and he would wipe each one off, smiling and singing his way through the day.

Finally, they became so ashamed of themselves that they called him in one day and said, "We want you to know that we're never going to play tricks on you again. Your attitude has been outstanding."

He asked, "You mean no more nailed shoes to floor?"

"No more."

"You mean no more grease on stove knobs?"

"No more."

"Okay then, no more spit in soup," he responded with a smile and a shrug.

Do you suppose we can keep an optimistic attitude without "spitting in the soup"?

Three Steps Forward, Two Steps Back

*Those who achieve excellence
are faithful in the details of life.*

EXCEL

*Excellence Inspires*

~

*L*eonardo da Vinci was once at work for a long period of time on a great masterpiece. He had labored long to create this work of art, and it was near completion. Standing near him was a young student who spent much of his time with his mouth open, amazed at the master with the brush. Just before finishing the painting, da Vinci turned to the young student and gave him the brush and said, "Now, you finish it." The student protested and backed away, but da Vinci said, "Will not what I have done inspire you to do your best?"

~ Swindoll's Ultimate Book of Illustrations

## Excellence of Mind and Will

~

First, excellence starts in the mind. It has to do with the way we think about God, ourselves, and others. Then it grows into the way we think about business, the way we think about dating, the way we think about marriage and the family.

Second, excellence has to do with the will. Disciplining the eyes, the ears, the hands, the feet. Keeping moral tabs on ourselves, refusing to let down the standards. People of excellence know how to turn right thinking into action—even when insistent feelings don't agree.

~ Living Above the Level of Mediocrity

*Something to Think About*

~

ince our choice of attitude is so important, our minds need fuel to feed on. Philippians 4:8 gives us a good place to start: "Finally, brethren, whatever is true, whatever is honorable, whatever is right, whatever is pure, whatever is lovely, whatever is of good repute, if there is any excellence and if anything worthy of praise, let your mind dwell on these things."

Good advice. "Let your mind dwell on these things." Fix your attention on these six specifics in life:

➤ Not unreal far-fetched dreams, but things that are *true*, real, valid.

➤ Not cheap, flippant, superficial stuff, but things that are *honorable*; i.e., worthy of respect.

➤ Not things that are wrong and unjust, critical and negative, but that which is *right*.

➤ Not thoughts that are carnal, smutty, and obscene, but that which is *pure* and wholesome.

➤ Not things that
prompt arguments
and defense in
others, but
those that
are *lovely*,
agreeable,
attractive,
winsome.

➤ Not slander, gossip, and
put-downs, but information
of *good report*, the kind that builds
up and causes grace to flow.

~ **Strengthening Your Grip**

Only by letting God reign in your life

can you experience true excellence.

*Free to Soar!*

~

I'm sure it comes as no surprise to most of us that we act out precisely what we take in. In other words, *we become what we think.* Long before that familiar line founds its way into Psychology 101 and hyped-up sales meetings, the Bible included it in one of its ancient scrolls; it just said it in a little different way: "For as he thinks within himself, so he is" (Proverbs 23:7).

The secret of living a life of excellence is merely a matter of thinking thoughts of excellence. It's a matter of programming our minds with the kind of information that will set us free.

Free to be all God meant us to be.

Free to soar!

~ Living Above the Level of Mediocrity

## Hardworking and Honest

~

A young fellow rushed into a gas station to use the pay phone. The manager overheard his telephone conversation as he asked: "Sir, could you use a hardworking, honest young man to work for you?" [pause] "Oh . . . you've already got a hardworking, honest young man? Well, thanks anyway!"

The boy hung up the phone with a smile. Humming to himself, he began to walk away, obviously happy.

"How can you be so cheery?" asked the eavesdropping manager. "I thought the man you talked to already had someone and didn't want to hire you."

The young fellow answered, "Well, you see I *am* the hardworking young man. I was just checking up on my job!"

If you called your boss, disguised your voice, and asked about your job, what do you think would be his answer?

~ Living Beyond the Daily Grind

A society that scorns excellence

in plumbing because it's a humble

occupation and promotes shoddy

philosophy because it's exalted,

has neither good plumbing nor

good philosophy. Neither its pipes

nor its theories will hold water.

JOHN GARDNER

# A Radical Renewal

~

We are like tiny islands of truth surrounded by a sea of paganism, but we launch our ship every day. We can't live or do business in this world without rubbing shoulders with those driven by the world's desires. God calls very few to be monks in a monastery. So we must make a practical decision not to be conformed while we are in the system, and at the same time, we must make a radical decision to give God the green light to transform our minds.

When a grub becomes a butterfly, there has been a metamorphosis, a radical transformation.

When a tadpole becomes a frog, there has been a transformation.

When the real Christ expresses Himself through our lives, . . . what occurs is nothing short of a striking, radical transformation. And how does it occur? "By the renewing of your mind." In order for you and me to keep ourselves from conforming to the world, we must

have a renewed mind—that inner part of our being where we decide who we are and where we stand.

At the deepest level, even though the majority may not want to admit it, most people are conformists. That is why it is correctly termed a radical decision. Only a radically different mindset can equip folks like us to stand alone when we're outnumbered.

〜 Living Above the Level of Mediocrity

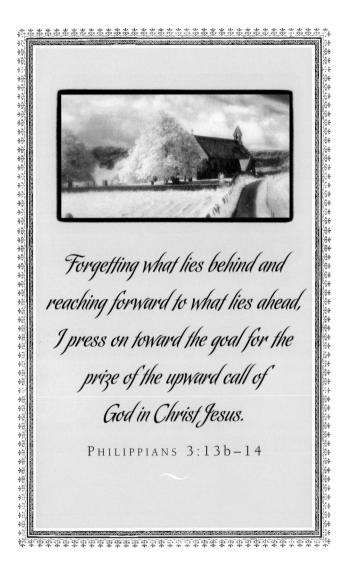

*Forgetting what lies behind and reaching forward to what lies ahead, I press on toward the goal for the prize of the upward call of God in Christ Jesus.*

PHILIPPIANS 3:13b–14

*A Quest for Excellence*

"*Reaching forward to what lies ahead.*" Paul could have been thinking of a chariot racer standing in that small two-wheeled cart with long, leather reins in his hands, leaning forward to keep his balance. Can you picture it?

The analogy is clear. In this race called life, we are to face forward, anticipating what lies ahead, ever stretching and reaching, making life a passionate, adventurous quest.

What is your particular quest? For what are you leaning forward? There is something wonderfully exciting about reaching into the future with excited anticipation, and those who pursue new adventures through life stay younger, think better, and laugh louder!

~ Laugh Again

*A Standard of Excellence*

~

xcellence requires one hundred percent all of the time.

Ever tracked the consequences of "almost but not quite"? Thanks to some fine research by Natalie Gabal, I awoke to a whole new awareness of what would happen if 99.9 percent were considered good enough. If that were true, then this year alone . . . 2,000,000 documents would be lost by the IRS; 12 babies would be given to the wrong parents each day; 291 pacemaker operations would be performed incorrectly; 20,000 incorrect drug prescriptions would be written; 114,500 mismatched pairs of shoes would be shipped (just to cite a few examples.)

~ The Finishing Touch

*Wisdom for Life*

~

As helpful as an education may be, reading widely or traveling broadly, or even being mentored by the brightest, none of that will automatically result in wisdom. It is not found in textbooks. Or discoveries. Or inventions. Or in some guru's mind. Seeking wisdom through human effort is a waste of time.

Allow me to offer a simple definition of wisdom. Wisdom is looking at life from God's point of view. You look at difficulties and tests as God looks at them. You look at family life as God looks at it. You interpret current events as God would interpret them.

~ *Job: A Man of Heroic Endurance*

*Three Questions of Discipleship*

~

1. As you think through the major decisions you have recently made (during the past six to eight months), have they pleased the Lord or fed your ego?

2. Have you begun to take your personal goals and desires before the Lord for His final approval?

3. Are you really willing to change those goals if, while praying about them, the Lord should lead you to do so?

Discipleship refuses to let us skate through life tossing around a few religious comments while we live as we please. It says, "There can be no more important relationship to you than the one you have with Jesus Christ." And it also says, "When you set forth your goals and desires in life, say no to the things that will only stroke your ego, and yes to the things that will deepen your commitment to Christ."

~ Strengthening Your Grip

As far as God is concerned, a

consistent godly life is well-pleasing.

As far as you are concerned,

it is an act of worship.

*God has not only created each of us as distinct individuals,*
*He also uses us in significant ways.*

CONFI

*Choose an Attitude of*

# DENCE

*Confidence Goes
Against the Flow*

~

everal years ago I met a gentleman who
served on one of Walt Disney's original
advisory boards. What amazing stories he
told! I especially appreciated the man's sharing with me
how Disney responded to disagreement. He said that
Walt would occasionally present some unbelievable,
extensive dream he was entertaining. Almost without
exception, the members of his board would gulp, blink,
and stare back at him in disbelief, resisting even the
thought of such a thing. But unless *every member resisted
the idea*, Disney usually didn't pursue it. Yes, you read
that correctly. The challenge wasn't big enough to merit
his time and creative energy unless everyone else was
unanimously in disagreement! Is it any wonder Disney
World became a reality?

~ Living Above the Level of Mediocrity

*Courage and Confidence*

ou will find a common dichotomy in life. Those who don't have vision or determination, and refuse to dream the impossible, are *always* in the majority.

Therefore they will always take the vote. They will always outshout and outnumber those who walk by faith and not by sight, those who are seeking the kingdom of God and His righteousness. Those who choose to live by sight will always outnumber those who live by faith.

To walk by faith requires courage. It requires the audacity to stand alone and challenge the majority to trust God.

*Living Above the Level of Mediocrity*

## Keep a Keen Focus

~

et this straight and never forget it: You will not stand alone when outnumbered or stand tall when tested or stand firm when discouraged if your focus remains on the odds. Your eyes must be trained on the Lord.

It's helpful for us to remember that our eyes are focused on one of four places at all times:

on our circumstances,

on others,

on ourself,

or on the Lord.

If they focus on one of the first three and not on the Lord, we will drift and ultimately fail. We must cultivate a keen focus on the Lord, not on the odds.

~ Living Above the Level of Mediocrity

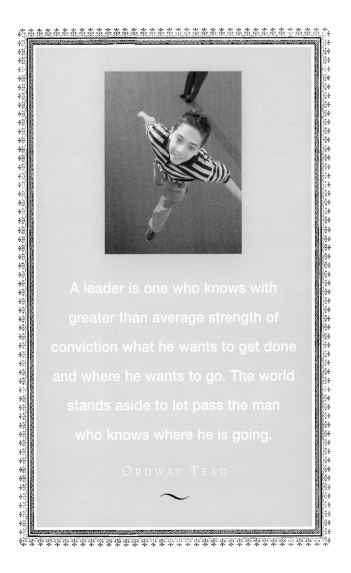

A leader is one who knows with greater than average strength of conviction what he wants to get done and where he wants to go. The world stands aside to let pass the man who knows where he is going.

ORDWAY TEAD

*"Good Job!"*

~

There are times we need to tell ourselves, "Good job!" when we know that is true. I smile as I write this to you, but I must confess that occasionally I even say to myself, "That's *very* good, Swindoll," when I am pleased with something I've done. That isn't conceited pride, my friend. It's acknowledging in words the feelings of the heart. The Lord knows that we hear more than enough internal put-downs! Communicating in times of leisure includes self-affirmation, acknowledging, of course, that God ultimately gets the glory. After all, He's the One who makes the whole experience possible.

~ *Strengthening Your Grip*

Only you can determine

your choice of attitude.

Choose wisely . . .

choose carefully . . .

choose confidently!

## Confidence in God's Perfect Plan

A sculptor was asked how he could carve a lion's head out of a large block of marble. "I just chip away everything that doesn't look like a lion's head," was his reply. God works away in our being and chips away everything that doesn't look like Christ—the impatience, the short temper, the pride. He's shaping us into His image. That's His predetermined plan. And He's committed to it. Nothing we can do will dissuade Him from that plan. He is relentless. . . .

Who would have guessed five years ago that you'd be doing what you're doing right now? Not one of us. And I have news for you. You have no idea what the next five years will bring. The future is just as uncertain and exciting and full of risk and wonder as the past five years. But whatever that future brings is also absolute, immutable, unconditional, and in complete harmony with God's nature and plans.

~ The Mystery of God's Will

## A Great Attitude

~

The only way to find happiness in the grind of life is *by faith*. A faith-filled life means all the difference in how we view everything around us. It affects our attitudes toward people, toward circumstances, toward ourselves. Only then do our feet become swift to do what is right.

You say you want to be considered great some day? Here's the secret: Walk by faith, trusting God to renew your attitude.

~ Joseph: A Man of Integrity & Forgiveness

God is not only good all the time,

He is in control all the time.

*Purpose in God's Presence*

~

*From everlasting to everlasting, Thou art God.*
PSALM 90:2

rom my yesterday to my tomorrow—God.
From the little involvements to the big ones—
God. From the beginning of school to the end
of school—God.

From the assignments that will never make the
headlines (which seem mere busy work) all the way
to those things that gain international attention—God.

As I go from the vanishing point of yesterday to
the vanishing point of tomorrow and find that God is
present, then there is not a place in the entire scope
of my everyday existence where God is not there. . . .
There is purpose, there is meaning in the presence of
God. Even in the things that seem to be pointless,
insignificant, trivial.

~ Living Above the Level of Mediocrity

*Christ Is Our Confidence*

~

*I am confident of this very thing, that He who began a good work in you will perfect it until the day of Christ Jesus.*
PHILIPPIANS 1:6

How do we live with worry and stress and fear?

Let me be downright practical and tell you what I do. First I remind myself early in the morning and on several occasions during the day, "God, You are at work, and You are in control. And, Lord God, You know this is happening. You were there at the beginning, and You will bring everything that occurs to a conclusion that results in Your greater glory in the end." Then (and *only* then!) I relax. From that point on, it really doesn't matter all that much what happens. It is in God's hands.

~ Laugh Again

God knows the way you take,

and it's not without purpose.

*What a Way to Live!*

~

When Christ becomes our central focus—our reason for existence—confidence replaces our anxiety as well as our fears and insecurities. This cannot help but impact three of the most prevalent joy stealers in all of life.

1. *He broadens the dimensions of our circumstances.* This gives us new confidence. Limitations become a challenge rather than a chore.

2. *He delivers us from preoccupation with others.* Other people's opinions, motives, and criticisms no longer seem all that important.

3. *He calms our fears regarding ourselves and our future.* This provides a burst of fresh hope on a daily basis.

When we arrive at dilemmas in life and are unable to decipher the right direction to go, if we hope to maintain our confidence in the process, we must (repeat *must*) allow the Lord to be our Guide, our Strength, our Wisdom—our all! It is easy to read those words, but so tough to carry through on them. When we do, however, it is nothing short of remarkable how peaceful and happy we can remain. The pressure is on His shoulders, the responsibility is on Him, the ball is in His court.

What a way to live!

~ Laugh Again

# Just the Beginning

~

More often than not, when something looks like it's the absolute *end*, it is really the *beginning*.

Think of the cross. The Roman officials applauded. The Jewish officials rejoiced. "Finally, we got rid of him, that troublemaker! We're glad that's over." Yet three days later, He was alive again. What seemed like an ending was only the beginning.

~ Esther: A Woman of Strength & Dignity

*Every day you can find at least one thing to laugh about.*

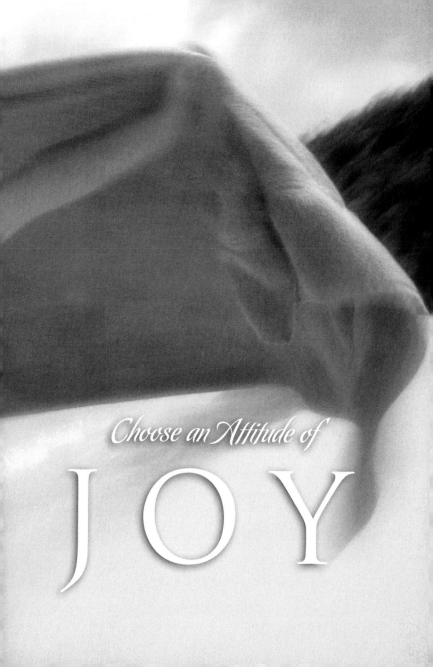

Choose an Attitude of

# JOY

# A Good Sense of Humor Helps

~

One of the best ways I know to have a joyful attitude is to have a good sense of humor. Turn the bad times into a little fun.

Years ago when our young family was living in Texas, we planned for months to go to a state park for a camping vacation We looked forward to it, but before we left we prayed, "Lord, whatever happens, we're going to have a good time."

It was a good thing we prayed that, because the place we stayed at was a rat hole. There were wall-to-wall people. It was hot—the weather was terrible! It was a great disappointment. We spent one night with spiders and scorpions, laughed it off, and headed back home. On the way, we stopped off at another state park where there wasn't a soul. I still can't understand it. We checked in and spent almost two full weeks in a place that was marvelously quiet and delightful, unseasonably cool and picturesque.

God seems to reward us with good, delightful experiences when we move with joy through the less-than-delightful times. The choice is ours.

— Three Steps Forward, Two Steps Back

Outrageous Joy!

~

*I* know of no greater need today than the need for joy. Unexplainable, contagious joy. Outrageous joy!

Someone once asked Mother Teresa what the job description was for anyone who might wish to work alongside her in the grimy streets and narrow alleys of Calcutta. Without hesitation she mentioned only two things: the desire to work hard and a joyful attitude. It has been my observation that both of those qualities are rare.

~ Laugh Again

*Feast on Cheer*

~

*A cheerful heart has a continual feast*
PROVERBS 15:15

sn't that a delightful way to put it? A cheerful heart serves the rest of the body (and others) a "continual feast." And what a sumptuous banquet! A well-developed sense of humor reveals a well-balanced personality. . . . The ability to get a laugh out of everyday situations is a safety valve. It rids us of tensions and worries that could otherwise damage our health. You think I'm exaggerating the benefits? If so, maybe you've forgotten another proverb: "A joyful heart is good medicine, but a broken spirit dries up the bones" (Prov. 17:22).

~ *Living Above the Level of Mediocrity*

## Rejoice in God's Gifts

D o you have eyesight? It's a gift. Do you have a good mind? It's a gift. How about dexterity in your fingers? Or special skills that allow you to work in your occupation? Do you have leadership abilities that cause others to follow? A good

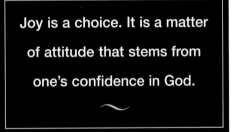

Joy is a choice. It is a matter of attitude that stems from one's confidence in God.

education? Do you have the ability to sell? These are all gifts from God's hand. Reflect on His numerous gifts to you. It will increase your joy. It will make you smile!

~ Living Above the Level of Mediocrity

A truly cheerful face comes

from  a joyful heart.

~

*Lighthearted Laughter*

~

A good sense of humor enlivens our discernment and guards us from taking everything that comes down the pike too seriously. By remaining lighthearted, by refusing to allow our intensity to gain the mastery of our minds, we remain much more objective. Ogden Nash believes this so strongly that he claimed that if the German people had had a sense of humor, they would never have let Adolf Hitler deceive them. Instead, the first time they saw some fellow goose-stepping and raising a stiff arm to shout, "Heil Hitler," they'd have keeled over in sidesplitting laughter.

~ *Laugh Again*

## What Are Your Goals?

~

When money is our objective, we must live in fear of losing it—which makes us paranoid and suspicious.

When fame is our aim, we become competitive lest others upstage us—which makes us envious.

When power and influence drive us, we become self-serving and strong-willed—which makes us arrogant.

And when possessions become our god, we become materialistic, thinking enough is never enough—which makes us greedy.

All these pursuits fly in the face of contentment . . . and joy.

~ Laugh Again

~

*Joyous people have the greatest opportunity to impact others positively, and they rarely leave a room the same way they found it.*

~

# Give Your Problems to God

~

*I*'m ready to believe that self-pity is "Private Enemy No.1." Things turn against us, making us recipients of unfair treatment, like innocent victims of a nuclear mishap. We neither expect it nor deserve it, and to make matters worse, it happens at the worst possible time. We're too hurt to blame.

Our natural tendency is to curl up in the fetal position and sing the silly little children's song: "Nobody loves me everybody hates me, I think I'll eat some worms." Which helps nobody. But what else can we do when the bottom drops out? Forgive me if this sounds too simplistic, but the only thing worth doing is usually the last thing we try doing—turning it over to our God, the Specialist, who has never yet been handed an impossibility He couldn't handle. Grab that problem by the throat and thrust it skyward! Don't let it steal your joy or dampen your confidence in God.

~ Strengthening Your Grip

*Create Space for Joy*

~

Our minds can be kept free of anxiety as we dump the load of our cares on the Lord in prayer. By getting rid of the stuff that drags us down, we create space for joy to take its place.

Think of it like this: Circumstances occur that could easily crush us. They may originate on the job or at home or even during the weekend when we are relaxing. Unexpectedly, they come. Immediately we have a choice to make . . . an attitude choice. We can hand the circumstance to God and ask Him to take control, or we can roll up our mental sleeves and slug it out. Joy awaits our decision.

~ *Strengthening Your Grip*

*Joy Wins the Red Ribbon*

~

Some Christians look like they've been baptized in lemon juice. Many have such long faces they could eat corn out of a Coke bottle! There are some exceptions, but therein lies the problem. Why are the joyful ones the exceptions?

If I read the Book correctly, joy is the runner-up virtue. If the "fruit of the spirit" is listed in the order of importance, love gets the blue ribbon, joy the red, right? If God awarded us medals, as they do in the Olympics, love would win the gold, joy the silver, and peace the bronze. I call that second-place finisher significant!

~ *Living Above the Level of Mediocrity*

There is nothing better than
a joyful attitude when we face the
challenges life throws at us.

~

> Enjoy a good belly laugh. You
> look fabulous when you laugh.

o you want to know the endless source of joy? Jesus Christ. Through Him alone we receive salvation—an act of love, fulfilled with joy, resulting in peace. Thanks be to God for His indescribable Gift. All that He is and all that He provides is enough to make me laugh out loud!

*Living Above the Level of Mediocrity*

*Integrity is not only the way one thinks*
*but even more the way one acts.*
TED ENGSTROM

# INTE

GRITY

## Don't Touch the Paint!

~

*I* have touched more wet paint just because somebody put a Wet Paint sign up, haven't you? I've thought that if they just wouldn't identify it as wet, I wouldn't touch it. But when it says Do Not Touch, I have to touch it. Something inside me forces my fingers onto wet paint. It's called sinful depravity. Signs don't help a bit.

One of my close friends told me about an unusual sign he saw in San Francisco. It read "*Try* to Keep off the Grass." My point? When you see a sign, the sign has no power whatsoever to make you obey. It certainly identifies the sin in us. And it intensifies the guilt when we ignore it, but it offers no power to restrain us.

What hope is there? The answer is found in Romans 5:20: "where sin increased, grace abounded all the more." Isn't that great! Grace overshadows sin; it outranks it and thereby brings hope.

~ The Grace Awakening

What are the marks of integrity?

> ➤ An excellent attitude
> ➤ Faithfulness and diligence at work
> ➤ Personal purity of the highest caliber
> ➤ Consistency in your walk with God.

~ Strengthening Your Grip

*Doing What Is Right—Regardless*

~

istory is full of accounts of individuals who made a difference. Think of Michelangelo, Brahms, Lincoln and Eisenhower. Think of the scientists, the explorers, the technological experts who have changed the course of history. Think of the courageous preachers who have stood alone in the gap and made a difference.

From Genesis to Revelation, we see God's hand on the lives of individuals who thought and said and did what was right—regardless—and as a result, history was made.

~ *Esther: A Woman of Strength & Dignity*

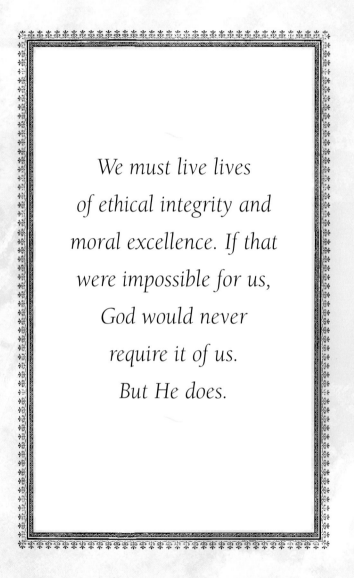

*We must live lives
of ethical integrity and
moral excellence. If that
were impossible for us,
God would never
require it of us.
But He does.*

*Stand Strong in Christ*

~

*M*arried or unmarried, divorced or remarried, man or woman, young or old, whatever your situation, no matter how alluring or pleasurable or momentarily delightful temptation looks, don't linger. Claim the supernatural strength that comes from knowing Jesus Christ and, operating under the control of His power, stand strong in His might. Right now, this very moment, determine to resist.

Otherwise, *you will yield.* It's only a matter of time.

~ Joseph: A Man of Integrity & Forgiveness

~

There is no counsel
like God's counsel.

No comfort like
His comfort.

No wisdom more
profound than the
wisdom of the
Scriptures.

~

## Do the Little Things Well

~

*I*f you want to be a person with a large vision, you must cultivate the habit of doing the little things well. That's when God puts iron in your bones! I'm talking about the way you fill out those detailed reports, the way you take care of those daily assignments, or the way you complete the tasks of home or dormitory or work or school. The test of my calling is not how well I do before the public on Sunday, it's how carefully I cover the bases Monday through Saturday when there's nobody to check up on me, when nobody is looking.

~ David: A Man of Passion & Destiny

*Play It Safe*

~

*I* have an attorney friend who works in conjunction
with the Federal Reserve Bank where stacks and
stacks and stacks of currency are kept and counted.
If you've never seen it, you can't imagine it!

He made the mistake of taking me there one afternoon.
We walked in together and went through a security check.
We walked down a narrow hallway and went through
another security check. We were on closed-circuit TV
cameras all the way. Behind a large section of bulletproof
glass are people who do nothing but count money. There
were stacks of crisp new hundred-dollar bills and stacks
of thousand-dollar bills.

I asked him, "How can they stand it behind there?"
(revealing something of my own depravity!).

He said, "Everything is fine if they remember their job
is only to count pieces of paper. If they begin to concentrate
on what those pieces of paper represent, then we have
problems."

Open doors to sin face us all each day. The person
centered on Christ and His righteousness says, "Nothing
doing," and willfully walks away.

~ Three Steps Forward, Two Steps Back

*He is a shield to those who walk in integrity, guarding the paths of justice.*

PROVERBS 2:7

*Integrity and Faith*

~

od magnifies HIS name when we are weak.
We don't have to be eloquent or strong or
handsome. We don't have to be beautiful or
brilliant or have
all the answers
to be blessed of
God. He honors
our faith. All He
asks is that we
trust Him, that

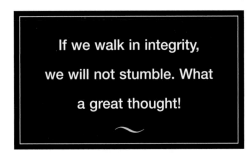

If we walk in integrity,
we will not stumble. What
a great thought!

~

we stand before Him in integrity and faith. God is just
waiting for us to trust Him.

~ David: A Man of Passion & Destiny

Walking in integrity is

the only way to live.

## Discernment and Discipline

~

To have the discernment it takes to refuse the sinful, faith must overshadow feelings.

My feelings say, "Run!" Faith says, "Stand still."

My feelings say, "Try it!" Faith says, "Stay away from it."

My feelings say, "Give it up. Throw in the towel." Faith says, "Hold on!"

We live in a day of feelings. "Whatever you *feel* like, get at it." The Academy Award-winning song about three of decades ago captured that philosophy with the words, "It can't be wrong, when it feels so right . . ." Oh, yes, it can! Faith says, "Hold it. You have come to a fork in the road. If you take that journey, you will buy into a lifestyle that is wrong. Stop. Back up. Look again."

That takes discernment and courage, but you can do it. God will give you the strength.

~ Moses: A Man of Selfless Dedication

Compromise never works.

*Christ Is Our Example*

~

A genuine disciple comes to the place where no major decision is made without a serious consideration of the question, "What would the Lord want me to do?" as opposed to, "How will this benefit me?" That kind of thinking is rare these days. Driven by our pride and stroked

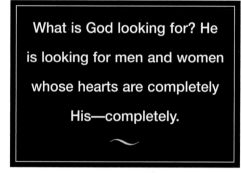

What is God looking for? He is looking for men and women whose hearts are completely His—completely.

~

by the endless flow of books (not to mention the media blitz) urging us on to find ourselves and please ourselves and satisfy ourselves and "be our own persons," we tend to recoil when we run upon advice like "Take up your cross and follow Me."

~ Strengthening Your Grip

*An Extinct Species*

~

Those who have integrity possess one of the most respected virtues in all of life.

Furthermore, they stand out in any office or school or community. If you can be trusted, whether alone or in a crowd . . . if you are truly a person of your word and convictions, you are fast becoming an extinct species.

~ *Strengthening Your Grip*

*Nothing great was ever
achieved without enthusiasm.*
RALPH WALDO EMERSON

# ENTH

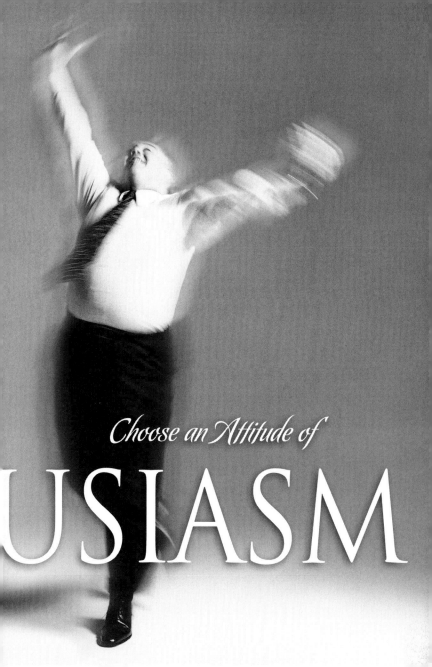

*Choose an Attitude of*

# USIASM

# You Are Special!

~

Possessions of the powerful, wealthy, or famous, no matter how common, can become extremely valuable, even priceless. Napoleon's toothbrush sold for $21,000. Can you imagine—paying thousands of dollars for someone's cruddy old toothbrush? Hitler's car sold for over $150,000. Winston Churchill's desk, a pipe owned by C. S. Lewis, sheet music handwritten by Beethoven, a house once owned by Ernest Hemingway. At the Sotheby's auction of Jackie Kennedy Onassis's personal belongings, her fake pearls sold for $211,500. Not because the item itself was worthy but because it once belonged to someone significant.

Are you ready for a surprise? We fit that bill too. Think of the value of something owned by God. What incredible worth that bestows on us, what inexplicable destiny. We are "a people for God's own possession" (1 Pet. 2:9).

We've been bought with a price. We belong to Him. That's enough to bring enthusiasm to anyone's life!

~ Hope Again

If one advances confidently in the direction
of his dreams, and endeavors to live the
life which he has imagined, he will
meet with a success unexpected
in common hours.

HENRY DAVID THOREAU

See Above and Beyond

~

hen I think of *vision*, I have in mind the ability to see above and beyond the majority. I am reminded of the eagle, whose eyes have eight times as many visual cells per cubic centimeter as a human. This translates into rather astounding abilities. For example, flying at 600 feet elevation, an eagle can spot an object the size of a dime moving through six-inch grass. The same creature can see three-inch fish jumping in a lake five miles away. Eagle-like people can envision what most would miss.

~ Living Above the Level of Mediocrity

*The Stuff of Leadership*

~

reams are the stuff of which leaders are made. If you don't dream, your leadership is seriously limited. I have a close friend who leads an organization that is admired and appreciated by many. He sets aside one day every month to do nothing but pray and dream. I am not surprised that his organization is considered a pacesetter.

~ *Living Above the Level of Mediocrity*

*Enthusiasm*

~

nthusiasm. Great word, *enthusiasm*. Its Greek original is *éntheos*, "God in." It is the ability to see God in a situation, which makes the event exciting. Something happens to our vision that is almost magical when we become convinced that God our heavenly

> **Wisdom says, do all you can within your strength, then trust God to do what you cannot do.**
>
> ~

Father is involved in our activities and is applauding them.

~ *Living Above the Level of Mediocrity*

*What Are Your Dreams?*

~

ost of us don't dream enough. If someone were to ask you, "What are your dreams for this year? What are your hopes, your agenda? What are you trusting God for?" could you give a specific answer? I don't have in mind just occupational objectives or goals . . . although there's nothing wrong with those. But what about the kind of dreaming that results in character building, the kind that cultivates God's righteousness and rulership in your life?

~ *Living Above the Level of Mediocrity*

A Few Ideas About Dreams

➤ Dreams are specific, not general.

➤ Dreams are personal, not public. God doesn't give any one else my dreams on a public computer screen for others to read. He gives them to me personally. They're intimate images and ideas.

➤ Dreams can easily appear to others as extreme and illogical. If you share your dreams with the crowd, they'll probably laugh at you because you can't make logical sense out of them.

➤ Dreams are often accompanied by a strong desire to fulfill them.

➤ Dreams are always outside the realm of the expected. Sometimes they're downright shocking.

➤ A common response when you share a dream is, "You've gotta be kidding! Are you serious?"

Living Above the Level of Mediocrity

*Living Above Life's Circumstances*

⁓

oseph was seventeen when he was thrown into the pit and began his long journey through affliction. He was thirty years old before he stood before Pharaoh and things began looking up in his life. Pause and consider—from ages seventeen to thirty—thirteen *long years*. Thirteen years since the bottom dropped out of his life. Thirteen years before things changed for the better.

Yet when I read the Genesis account and try to locate any sign of discouragement on Joseph's part, I cannot find it.

Joseph was a man who lived above the drag of despair. He lived far above his circumstances. His long period of affliction did not discourage him.

⁓ Joseph: A Man of Integrity & Forgiveness

Once you've decided to live differently,

let God be your guide and hang tough—

follow your dreams with determination.

~

God's Greater Glory

~

When a musician has a fine composition placed before her, that music is not the musician's masterpiece; it is the composer's gift to the musician. But it then becomes the task of the musician to work it out, to give it sound and expression and beauty as she applies her skills to the composition. When she does, the composition reaches it completed purpose and thrills the hearts of her listeners.

Spiritually speaking, the ultimate goal or purpose of our lives is "His good pleasure" (Phil. 2:13). Our lives are to be lived for God's greater glory—not our own selfish desires.

Are we left to do so all alone? Is it our task to gut it out, grit our teeth, and do His will? Not at all. Here's the balance: *God is at work in us!* He is the one who gives us strength and empowers our diligence. As He pours His power into us, we do the things that bring Him pleasure.

~ Laugh Again

*I can do all things through Him who strengthens me.*
PHILIPPIANS 4:13

onsider Paul's statement. Whatever we may substitute for "Christ" fails to fit the statement. Let's try several.

"I can do all things through *education*." No.

"I can do all things through *money*." No.

"I can do all things through *success*." No.

"I can do all things through *friends*." No.

"I can do all things through *positive thinking*." No.

Nothing else fits . . . only Christ. Why? Because nothing and no one else is able to empower us and provide the strength we need.

~ Laugh Again

CORD

*Life is a lot like a coin;*
*you can spend it any way you wish,*
*but you can spend it only once.*

*Choose an Attitude of*

IALITY

*Thoughtful and Kind*

~

The children worked long and hard on their little cardboard shack. It was to be a special spot—a clubhouse, where they could meet together, play, and have fun. Since a clubhouse has to have rules, they came up with three:

1. Nobody act big.

2. Nobody act small.

3. Everybody act medium.

Not bad theology!

In different words, God says the very same thing: "Let each of you regard one another as more important than himself" (Phil. 2:3).

Just "act medium." Believable. Honest, human, thoughtful, and down-to-earth.

~ Day by Day with Charles Swindoll

Godliness is not skin deep.
It is something below the
surface of a life, deep down
in the realm of an attitude.

~

*The wise in heart will be*
*called discerning, and sweetness*
*of speech increases persuasiveness.*

PROVERBS 16:21

## Who Needs Our Help?

~

God commands that we reach out, accept, and affirm one another. This means that we consciously resist the strong current of the stream we are in . . . the one that dictates all those excuses:

> "I'm just too busy."
> "It's not worth the risk."
> "I don't really need anyone."
> "If I reach out, I'll look foolish."

We have been deluded into believing that we really shouldn't concern ourselves with being our brother's keeper. After all, we have time pressures and work demands (that relentless, fierce determination to be number one), not to mention, anxieties prompted by economic uncertainty. And who really needs our help anyway? I'll tell you who—just about every person we meet, that's who.

~ Strengthening Your Grip

## Giving Encouragement

~

he people we meet every day are harassed by demands and deadlines; bruised by worry, adversity, and failure; broken by disillusionment; and defeated by sin. They live somewhere between dull discouragement and sheer panic. Even Christians are not immune! We may give off this "I've got it all together" air of confidence, but realistically, we also struggle, lose our balance, slip and slide, tumble, and fall flat on our faces.

All of us need encouragement—somebody to believe in us. To reassure and reinforce us. To help us pick up the pieces and go on. To provide us with increased determination in spite of the odds.

When you stop to analyze the concept, "encourage" takes on new meaning. It's the act of inspiring others with renewed courage, spirit, or hope. When we encourage others we spur them on, we stimulate and affirm them.

~ Strengthening Your Grip

Encouragement is like an

oasis in the desert.

~

*We Need Each Other*

~

obody is a whole chain. Each one is a link. But take away one link and the chain is broken.

Nobody is a whole team. Each one is a player. But take away one player and the game is forfeited.

The beautiful part about encouragement is this: Anybody can do it.

~

Nobody is a whole orchestra. Each one is a musician. But take away one musician and the symphony is incomplete. . . .

You guessed it. We need each other. You need someone and someone needs you. Isolated islands we're not.

~ The Finishing Touch

*Cordiality Allows for Differences*

~

isagreements are inevitable. There will always be opposing viewpoints and a variety of perspectives on most subjects. Tastes differ as well as preferences. That is why they make vanilla and chocolate and strawberry ice cream, why they build Fords and Chevys, Chryslers and Cadillacs, Hondas and Toyotas. That is why our nation has room for Democrats and Republicans, conservatives and liberals—and moderates. The tension is built into our system. It is what freedom is all about, including religious freedom.

I am fairly firm in my theological convictions, but that doesn't mean you (or anyone) must agree with me. All this explains why we must place so much importance on leaving "wobble room" in our relationships. One's theological persuasion may not bend, but one's involvements with others must.

~ The Grace Awakening

A Steady Stream of Love

An insightful person once said, "We are most like God when we forgive." Every one of us can blame somebody for something that has happened in our lives. But don't waste your time. What we need most is a steady stream of love flowing among us. Love that quickly forgives, willingly overlooks, and refuses to take offense.

Some people are so easy to love that you just naturally fall into their arms. But others are so hard to love, you have to work overtime at it. Yet even they need our love, perhaps more than the others.

~ Hope Again

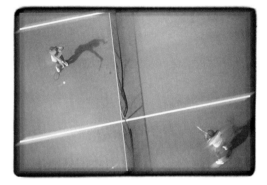

*Release Resentment*

~

If you are resentful of the way someone has treated you, if you are holding it against that person, hoping you can retaliate or get back, you need to ask God to free you from that bondage. The secret, plain and simple? Forgiveness! Claim God's power to forgive through Jesus Christ. Begin by asking His forgiveness for excusing and cultivating that deep root of bitterness within your own heart. Ask him to expose it in all its ugliness and put it to death. Jesus Christ, who went through hell for you, can give you the power you need to overcome the worst kind of condition in your life.

~ David: A Man of Passion & Destiny

## A Magnanimous Attitude

~

Why was Joseph considered great? He certainly wasn't superhuman. He never walked on water. He had no halo.

Then, why was Joseph so great? He was great because of his faith in God, which manifested itself in a magnanimous attitude toward others and his magnificent attitude toward difficulties. A strong faith leads to a good attitude.

~ Joseph: A Man of Integrity & Forgiveness

*How's Your Serve?*

~

S omeone said, "Business is a lot like the
game of tennis. Those who don't serve well
end up losing."

Do you serve under someone else's authority?
How's your attitude, toward that person? Having the
right attitude can be especially tough if the person
to whom you answer is a difficult individual or an
incompetent leader or one whose weaknesses you
know all too well. This is not only a test of your loyalty,
but a test of your Christian maturity.

~ *Joseph, A Man of Integrity & Forgiveness*

*Let me give you
a simple tip: We
cannot be right with
God until we are
right with others.*

*In spite of our high-tech
world and efficient
procedures, people
remain the essential
ingredient of life.*

## Freedom to Forgive

~

*orgiveness* and *bitterness*. Without the first you'll limp through life with the second.

Misunderstanding can breed deep-seated bitterness, which doesn't easily go away. Forgiveness must occur if you ever hope to be free of your painful past. It doesn't mean you agree. It doesn't necessarily mean you now have a close relationship with your offender. But it does mean you let it go . . . forever. And yes, to forgive *does* mean to forget. Bitterness deposits dangerous germs in our memory banks. It can cause disease that lingers and robs us of joy and peace. So you must forgive and forget. Bitterness replaces forgiveness, or forgiveness erases bitterness. They cannot coexist.

~ Getting Through the Tough Stuff

*As Gracious as Christ*

~

We can learn to be as gracious as Christ. And since we can, we must . . . not only in our words and in great acts of compassion and understanding but in small ways as well.

Sir Edward C. Burne-Jones, the prominent nineteenth-century English artist, went to tea at the home of his daughter. As a special treat his young granddaughter was allowed to come to the table. But she misbehaved, and her mother made her stand in the corner with her face to the wall. Sir Edward, a well-trained grandfather, did not interfere with his grandchild's training, but the next morning he arrived at his daughter's home with paints and palette. He went to the wall where the little girl had been forced to stand, and there he painted pictures—a kitten chasing its tail, lambs in a field, goldfish swimming. He decorated the wall . . . for his granddaughter's delight. If she had to stand in the corner again, at least she would have something wonderful to look at!

~ The Grace Awakening

When I have a wrong attitude,
I look at life humanly.
When I have a right attitude,
I look at life divinely.

PERSEV

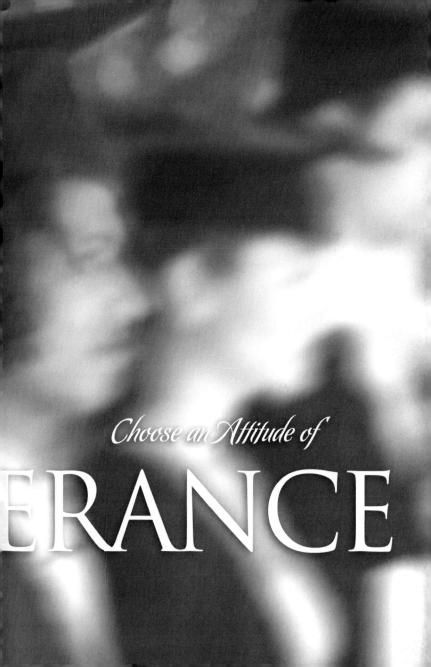

*Choose an Attitude of*

ERANCE

# I'm Glad They Didn't Quit

~

All of us are surrounded by and benefit from the results of someone's perseverance. Let me name a few:

➤ Above my head is a bright electric light. Thanks, Tom.

➤ On my nose are eyeglasses that enable me to focus. Thanks, Ben.

➤ In my driveway is a car ready to take me wherever I choose to steer it. Thanks, Henry.

➤ Across my shelves are books full of interesting and carefully researched pages. Thanks, authors.

My list could go on and on. So could yours.

Because some cared enough to dream, to pursue, to follow through and complete their quest, our lives are more comfortable, more stable.

That's enough to spur me on. How about you?

~ Day by Day with Charles Swindoll

*Persevere for God's Purpose*

~

When we awaken in the morning, we choose the attitude that will ultimately guide our thoughts and actions through the day. I'm convinced our best attitudes emerge out of a clear understanding of our own identity, a clear sense of our divine mission, and a deep sense of God's purpose for our lives. That sort of God-honoring attitude encourages us to press on, to focus on the goal, to respond in remarkable ways to life's most extreme circumstances.

~ Paul: A Man of Grace & Grit

I'll be frank with you.

I know of no more valuable

technique in the pursuit

of successful living

than sheer, dogged

determination.

~

*Determination Makes for Greatness*

often meet people who have been misled, thinking that success depends solely upon talent or brilliance or education. Some think it's getting the breaks, pulling the right strings, having the right personality, or being in the right place at the right time.

No, the thing that makes for greatness is determination, persisting in the right direction over the long haul, following your dream, staying at the task. Just as there is no such thing as instant failure, neither is there automatic or instant success. But success is the direct result of a process that is long, arduous, and often unappreciated by others. It also includes a willingness to sacrifice. But it pays off if you stay at the task.

— Living Above the Level of Mediocrity

## Paganini . . . and One String

The colorful, nineteenth-century showman and gifted violinist Nicolo Paganini was standing before a packed house, playing through a difficult piece of music. A full orchestra surrounded him with magnificent support. Suddenly one string on his violin snapped and hung gloriously down from his instrument. Beads of perspiration popped out on his forehead. He frowned but continued to play, improvising beautifully.

To the conductor's surprise, a second string broke. And shortly thereafter, a third. Now there were three limp strings dangling from Paganini's violin as the master performer completed the difficult composition on the one remaining string. The audience jumped to its feet and in good Italian fashion, filled the hall with shouts and screams, "Bravo! Bravo!" As the applause died down, the violinist asked the people to sit back down. Even though they knew there was no way they could expect an encore, they quietly sank back into their seats.

He held the violin high for everyone to see. He nodded at the conductor to begin the encore and then he turned back to the crowd, and with a twinkle in his eyes, he smiled and shouted, "Paganini . . . and one string!" He placed the single-stringed Stradivarious beneath his chin and played the final piece on *one* string as the audience shook their heads in silent amazement. "Paganini . . . and one string!" *And*, I might add, an attitude of fortitude!

∽ Strengthening Your Grip

*Do not fear, for I have redeemed you; I have called you by name; you are Mine!*

<small>ISAIAH 43:1b</small>

~

## God Has a Plan

I t's easy to lose your bearings in the storm. You can't find your way through the circumstances you face. Life rolls along fairly smoothly until suddenly the seas grow rough. Unseen problems occur. They were not in the forecast.

Those are treacherous moments when we reach the point of abandoning hope. At that difficult, gut-wrenching moment God says, "Don't be afraid, I have a plan."

Paul: A Man of Grace & Grit

## Standing Strong

~

Tucked away in Hebrews 11:27 is a two-word biography: ". . . he persevered." (NIV) The "he" refers to Moses. Moses was the one who hung tough, who refused to give in or give up, who decided that no amount of odds against him would cause him to surrender. He had staying power. Once Moses made up his mind, nothing would deter the man.

He endured, despite the contempt of Pharoah.

He endured, despite the stubbornness of the Hebrews who grumbled, blamed, complained, and rebelled.

He endured, despite the criticisms of his own sister and brother.

He endured despite disappointments.

Moses endured. How? By focusing his attention on "Him who is invisible" (Heb. 11:27). He fixed his heart and soul on the One who, alone, judges righteously. He continually reminded himself that his sole purpose in life was to please the Lord . . . to obey Him . . . to glorify Him.

Whatever it is you're facing, stand strong. Walk in quiet confidence, not veiled pride.

Be sure without being stubborn . . . full of truth balanced with grace.

〜 The Finishing Touch

I'm glad . . .

➤ that Edison didn't give up on the light bulb.

➤ that Luther refused to back down.

➤ that Michelangelo kept painting.

➤ that Lindbergh kept flying.

*Obstacle or Opportunity?*

~

eople who know who they are, who possess a clear sense of their mission, and who understand God's plan and purpose for their lives, are people who experience genuine fulfillment. That doesn't mean they don't face extreme obstacles. Rather, it means they have learned to face those challenges in ways that transform obstacles into opportunities. Rather than stumbling over them, they press on through them.

*The righteous will never be shaken.*

PROVERBS 10:29–30

~ From A Man of Grace & Grit

*Our Lord is searching for people who will make a difference, who will stand alone—stand tall, stand firm, stand strong!*

*Empowered to Persevere*

~

All the hoping and dreaming in the world won't make it possible for me to sit down at a piano and play a Beethoven sonata like Van Cliburn. Nice idea but an impossible notion. But if the world renowned pianist were somehow able to confer on me all the skill and brilliance of his ability, undergirded by his decades of study and practice and magnificent talent, perhaps I could pull it off. But make no mistake, that would require a transfer of Van Cliburn's musical genius into my very being. I would need his spirit within me, literally.

That's what we face in the Christian life. Christ has given us His power through the infilling presence of the Holy Spirit. The Holy Spirit indwells us when we turn to God through faith in His Son. No need to pray, fast, hope, shout, or plead for divine power. If you are a follower of Christ, you have Christ's power in you. The Holy Spirit literally resides within your being. The more you yield your life to Him, the more His power flows through you. He is there, ready and able to empower us. Is that great news or what?

~ Getting Through the Tough Stuff

*But if we hope for what we do not see,*

*with perseverance we wait eagerly for it.*

ROMANS 8:25

*Aim High!*

~

he world is full of folks who would quickly give up. They sit back with folded arms, deep frowns, and skeptical stares. Their determination is short-lived. Their favorite words are *"Why try? . . . Give up . . . We can't do that . . . Nobody ever does those things."* And they miss out on most of the action, to say nothing of all the fun!

But periodically we bump into a few refreshing souls, who have decided that they aren't going to live in the swamp of the status quo or run scared of being different. Those who aim high are strong-willed eagle types who refuse to be bothered by the negativism and skepticism of the majority. They never even use the words "Let's just quit!"

~ *Living Above the Level of Mediocrity*

*Don't Quit*

~

ou may be one who lives your life pursuing fame and fortune, depending on the applause of others. Bad plan. To begin with, fortune has shallow rules.

The winds of adversity can quickly blow it all away. Fame is as fickle as the last response from the crowd. Learn a dual lesson.

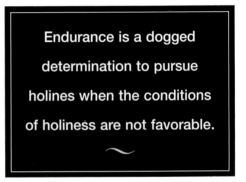

**Endurance is a dogged determination to pursue holines when the conditions of holiness are not favorable.**

~

When you're praised and applauded, don't pay any attention. When you're rejected and abused, don't quit.

~ Paul: A Man of Grace & Grit

*Cultivating Character*

~

In our nation of fast foods and quick fixes, the great hope of Americans is overnight change.

Many are too impatient to wait for anything and too lazy to work long and hard to make it happen. We want what we want when we want it, and the sooner the better—which explains our constant pursuit of hurry-up formulas. Everything from diet fads promising rapid weight loss to immediate financial success through clever schemes captures our fancy and gets our vote. Everybody, it seems, expects instant transformation.

But when it comes to the cultivation of character, I know of nothing that takes longer, is harder work, or requires greater effort.

~ Living Above the Level of Mediocrity

*Hanging Tough*

~

hen I think of *determination*, I think of inner fortitude, strength of character— being disciplined to remain consistent, strong, and diligent regardless of the odds or the demand.

Determination is hanging tough when the going gets rough. It means keeping a constant focus on God who is watching and smiling.

~ *Living Above the Level of Mediocrity*

*God is the Lord of good*
*days and bad days.*

*Hope makes a dismal today*
*bearable because it promises*
*a brighter tomorrow.*

~

*There is no quality more godlike than humility.*

# HUM

*Choose an Attitude of*

# ILITY

## Keeping Things in Perspective

~

A new member of British parliament took his eight-year-old daughter on a brief tour of his beloved London. They came to Westminster Abbey and the awesomeness of it struck the little girl. She stood looking way up at the columns and studying the beauty and grandeur of the ancient Gothic church. Her father was intrigued at her concentration. He looked down and said, "Sweetheart, what are you thinking about?

She said, "Daddy, I was thinking how big you seem at home and how small you look in here."

~ Swindoll's Ultimate Book of Illustrations

*A Servant Mentality*

~

*Do nothing from selfishness or empty conceit, but*
*with humility of mind regard one another as more*
*important than himself; do not merely look out for your*
*own personal interests, but also for the interests of others.*

PHILIPPIANS 2 : 3 – 4

umility is a mental choice we make, a
decision not to focus on self . . . me . . .
my . . . mine but on the other person. It's
a servant mentality. When we strengthen our grip on
attitudes, a great place to begin is with humility—
authentic and gracious unselfishness.

~ Strengthening Your Grip

*An Attitude of the Heart*

~

*Have this attitude in yourselves*
*which was also in Christ Jesus.*
PHILIPPIANS 2:5

umility is not how you dress, it in not the money you make, it is not where you live, it's not what you drive, it is not even how you look. We're never once commanded by God to "look" humble. Humility is an attitude. It is an attitude of the heart. An attitude of the mind. It is knowing your proper place. Never talking down or looking down because someone may be of a financial level less than yours. It is knowing your role and fulfilling it for God's glory and praise.

~ Esther: A Woman of Strength & Dignity

*True Humility*

⁓

he elder President Bush praised Ronald Reagan's humility in his eulogy. In 1981, Reagan was recovering from the gunshot wound he received during the assassination attempt. Just days after the surgery that repaired his life-threatening injuries, his aides discovered him on his hands and knees in his hospital room, wiping water from the floor. Bush said of Reagan, "He worried that his nurse would get in trouble."

I call that gracious act of humility strength of character. How rarely would we imagine our president on his hands and knees cleaning up his own mess. But that's true humility.

⁓ So, You Want to Be Like Christ?

Humility—the discipline of putting
others ahead of self, the choice
to value others above self—is,
at its core, a matter of faith.

~

*God Is Tops, I am Not*

othing is so welcome as true humility, which is nothing more than a realization of one's standing before God (He is tops, number one, preeminent) and a willingness to be cut down to

**Submission to the Father's will is the mark of genuine humility.**

size in order for Him to be exalted and glorified. Humility has learned the hard way that no person can operate in the flesh and produce any good thing, so it prevents us from trying.

*The Grace Awakening*

*A Christlike Attitude*

~

As I have pored over the Bible, looking for insights into Christ's life, I have been intrigued by His responses to others. How could any man be as patient as He was? How could He keep His cool under constant fire? How could He demonstrate so much grace, so much compassion, and at the same time so much determination? And when faced with the Pharisees' continued badgering and baiting, how could He restrain Himself from punching their lights out? As a man, He had all the emotions we have as human beings. What was it that gave Him the edge we so often lack? *It was His attitude.*

Which brings up a question: What is the most Christlike attitude on earth? Think before you answer too quickly. I am certain many would answer *love.* Others might say *patience. Grace* would also be a possibility. But as important as those traits may be, they are not the ones Jesus Himself referred to when He described Himself for the only time in Scripture . . .

"Take my yoke upon you, and learn from Me, for I am gentle and humble in heart. . . ." Matthew 11:29

The key words might be summed up in the one word, *unselfish*.

～ *Laugh Again*

*Putting Others First*

~

The way up is down. The place of highest exaltation, as we see in the Lord Jesus Christ, is a place of self-emptying humility. It's not a phony-baloney style of fake piety. It's true humility of mind. It's putting the other person first. It's sharing and sharing alike. It is giving up as well as building up. It is enjoying the pleasures of another's promotion. It is applauding God's hand in other lives. It is quickly forgetting one's own clippings. It is being like Christ.

~ *Esther: A Woman of Strength & Dignity*

Christlikeness is a journey,
not a destination. Plan on
a lifetime of travel.

~

*He Humbled Himself*

~

*Have this attitude in yourselves which was also in
Christ Jesus, who, although He existed in the form of
God, did not regard equality with God a thing to be grasped,
but emptied Himself, taking the form of a bond-servant,
and being made in the likeness of men. Being found in
appearance as a man, He humbled Himself by becoming
obedient to the point of death, even death on a cross.*

PHILIPPIANS 2:5–8

Maybe you have never stopped to think
about it but behind the scenes, it was an
attitude that brought the Savior down to
us. He deliberately chose to come among us because
He realized and valued our need. He placed a higher
significance on it than His own comfort and prestigious
position. In humility, He set aside the glory of heaven
and came to be among us. He refused to let His
position keep us at arm's length.

~ Strengthening Your Grip

## A Clear Vision

All whom God uses greatly are first hidden in the secret of His presence, away from the pride of man. It is there our vision clears. It is there the silt drops from the current of our life and our faith begins to grasp His arm.

Abraham waited for the birth of Isaac.

Moses didn't lead the Exodus until he was eighty.

Elijah waited beside the brook.

Noah waited 120 years for rain.

Paul was hidden away for three years in Arabia.

God is working while His people are waiting, waiting, waiting.

That's what's happening. For the present time, nothing. For the future, everything!

Joseph: A Man of Integrity & Forgiveness

When my attitudes are right, there's no barrier
too high, no valley too deep, no dream too
extreme, no challenge too great.

~

## The Limelight or the Shadows?

~

ather than racing into the limelight, we need to accept our role in the shadows.

Don't promote yourself. Don't push yourself to the front. Let someone else do that. Better yet, let God do that.

If you're great, trust me, the word will get out. You'll be found . . . in God's time. If you're necessary for the plan, God will put you in the right place at just the precise time.

~ Paul: A Man of Grace & Grit

*Selflessness*

~

ouglas Southall Freeman ends his four-volume work on Robert E. Lee with a touching scene. General Lee was wrinkled and gray and stooped over—very close to death—when a young mother came to see him with her infant cradled in her arms. When Lee reached out for her baby, she responded by placing the infant in Lee's still-strong arms. The great general looked deeply into the child's eyes and then slowly turned to the mother and said, "Teach him he must deny himself."

The path to greatness in the kingdom of God will lead you through the valley of selflessness. Christlike humility will emerge on its own.

~ So, You Want to Be Like Christ?

*Strength and Security*

~

*H*umility, isn't the result of having a poor self-image. True humility comes from a place of strength and inner security. Genuinely humble people who have a desire to seek the well-being of others are generally very secure people. They are fully aware of their gifts, their training, their experience, and all the attributes that make them successful at whatever they do. That security—that honest, healthy self-assessment—results in more than a humble constitution; it translates into actions that can be observed, actions that others will want to emulate.

~ So, You Want to Be Like Christ?

*I've never known anyone
who went bad because
he was too generous.*

# GENE

*Choose an Attitude of*

# ROSITY

## Satisfaction in Serving Others

~

My sister, Luci, told me about the time she visited with a famous opera singer in Italy. This woman owned a substantial amount of Italian real estate, a lovely home, and a yacht floating on the beautiful Mediterranean in a harbor below her villa. At one point, Luci asked the singer if she considered all this the epitome of success.

"Why, no!" the woman exclaimed, sounding a bit shocked.

"What is success then?"

"When I stand to perform, to sing my music, and I look out upon a public that draws a sense of fulfillment, satisfaction, and pleasure from my expression of this art, at that moment I know I have contributed to someone else's need. That to me describes success."

~ Hope Again

*Give Abundantly*

~

There's nothing in the world wrong with making a nice living. Nor is there anything wrong with being eminently wealthy if you earn and handle it correctly. But there's something drastically wrong when you keep it all to yourself! God gave it to you so you could, in turn, give it back to Him, to others—yes, in *abundance*. The only reason I can imagine for God's allowing anyone to make more than one needs is to be able to give more.

~ Living Above the Level of Mediocrity

*Greathearted Generosity*

∼

*"God loves a cheerful giver."*
2 CORINTHIANS 9:7

over for a moment over the key word,
*cheerful*. In Greek it is the term *hilaros*,
from which we get our word *hilarious*. It is
such an unusual word it appears nowhere else in all the
New Testament. . . . The sentence could be rendered,
"For the hilarious giver God prizes." Do you know why
He prizes the hilarious giver? Because the hilarious
giver gives so generously. He has no special possession
or gift or skill or amount of money that he grips tightly.
No, when the heart is full of joy, it is amazing how it
causes the pockets to turn inside out. A joyful heart
expresses itself in greathearted generosity.

∼ Living Above the Level of Mediocrity

Jesus says,
"Be a servant, give
to others!" Now that's
a philosophy anybody
can understand.

~

*Give Your Blessings Away*

~

I have a close pastor friend who traveled across the country for a week of meetings. The only problem was, his baggage didn't make it. As I recall, the bags went on to Berlin! He really needed a couple of suits. So he went down to the local thrift shop. When he told the clerk, "I'd like to get a couple of suits," the fellow smiled and said, "Good, we've got several. But you need to know they came from the local mortuary. They've all been cleaned and pressed, but they were used on stiffs. Not a thing wrong with 'em." My friend smiled and said, "That's fine. That's okay." So he hurriedly tried some on and bought a couple for about twenty-five bucks apiece. Great deal!

When he got back to his room, he began to get dressed for the evening's meeting. As he put one suit on, he discovered that there were no pockets. Both sides were all sewed up! Though surprised, he thought, *Why of course! Stiffs don't carry stuff with 'em!*

Since we can't take our earthly blessings with us, we might as well give them away!

~ *Living Above the Level of Mediocrity*

*True Riches*

~

t's foolish to trust in riches for security since they bring no lasting satisfaction. There are many things that no amount of money can buy. Think of it this way:

Money can buy medicine, but not health.

Money can buy a house, but not a home.

Money can buy companionship, but not friends.

Money can buy entertainment, but not happiness.

Money can buy food, but not an appetite.

Money can buy a bed, but not sleep.

Money can buy a crucifix, but not a Savior.

Money can buy the good life, but not eternal life.

God (alone) is able to supply us "with all things to enjoy." As Seneca, the Roman statesman once said: "Money has never yet made anyone rich."

~ Strengthening Your Grip

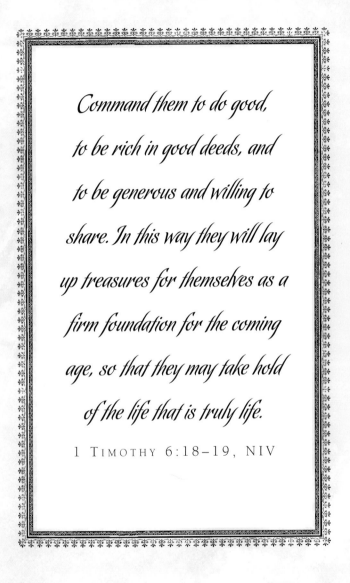

Command them to do good,
to be rich in good deeds, and
to be generous and willing to
share. In this way they will lay
up treasures for themselves as a
firm foundation for the coming
age, so that they may take hold
of the life that is truly life.

1 TIMOTHY 6:18–19, NIV

A Trademark of Generosity

ou have money? Release it, don't hoard it. Be a great-hearted person of wealth. Let generosity become your trademark. Be generous with your time, your efforts, your energy, your encouragement, and, yes, your money.

Do you know what will happen? Along with being enriched, knowing that you are investing in eternity, you will "take hold of the life that is truly life." You will go beyond "the good life" and enter into "the *true* life." There is a vast difference between the two.

Strengthening Your Grip

*Truly Unselfish*

~

Someone who is truly unselfish is generous with his or her time and possessions, energy and money. As that works its way out, it is demonstrated in various ways, such as thoughtfulness and gentleness, an unpretentious spirit, and servant-hearted leadership.

> ➤ When a husband is unselfish, he subjugates his own wants and desires to the needs of his wife and family.

> ➤ When a mother is unselfish, she isn't irked by having to give up her agenda or plans for the sake of her children.

> ➤ When an athlete is unselfish, it is the team that matters, not winning the top honors personally.

> ➤ When a Christian is unselfish, others mean more than self. Pride is given no place to operate.

~ Laugh Again

*Living in truth is
making the right choices.
The secret, of course,
is making the right
choices every day.*

*I don't see life divided
into public and private,
secular and sacred. It's all
an open place of service
before our God.*

*Shalom*

~

We live in a world where we take care of our own. We look out for number one. But God's plan encompasses everyone. Every nation. Every race. All cultures. Huge, highly developed countries, but not excluding the small, struggling ones. His message of *shalom* through faith in Christ is universal. Unlimited. Without prejudice. Vast!

~ Esther: A Woman of Strength & Dignity

*Helping Others*

~

ow do we create an unselfish attitude?
Three practical ideas come to mind:

➤ Never let selfishness or conceit be your motive.
*Never.*

➤ Always regard others as more important than
yourself.

➤ Don't limit your attention to your own personal
interests—include others.

Some may try to dissuade you from what may
appear to be an unbalanced, extremist position.
They may tell you that anyone who adopts this sort
of attitude is getting dangerously near self-flagellation
and a loss of healthy self-esteem. Nonsense! The goal
is that we become so interested in helping others reach
their highest good that we become self-forgetful in the
process.

~ Laugh Again

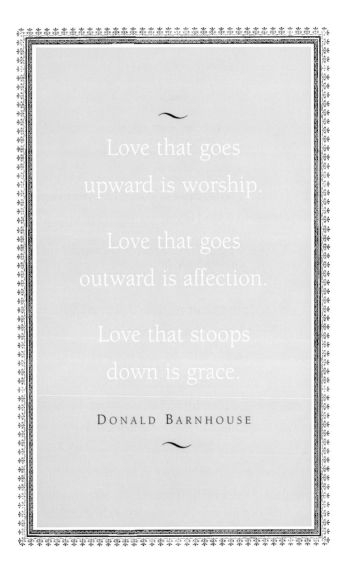

Love that goes
upward is worship.

Love that goes
outward is affection.

Love that stoops
down is grace.

DONALD BARNHOUSE

# Closing Thoughts

~

houghts are the thermostat that regulates what we accomplish in life. My body responds and reacts to the input from my mind. If I feed my mind upon doubt, disbelief, and discouragement, that is precisely the kind of day my body will experience. If I adjust my thermostat forward to thoughts filled with vision, vitality, and victory, I can count on that kind of day. . . .

Thoughts, positive or negative, grow stronger when fertilized with constant repetition. That may explain why so many who are gloomy and gray stay in that mood . . . and why those who are cheery and enthusiastic continue to be so.

There are many voices these days. Some are loud, many are persuasive, and a few are downright convincing. It can be confusing. If you listen long enough you will be tempted to throw your faith to the winds, look out for number one, let your glands be your guide, and choose what is best for you. Initially you will get a rush of pleasure and satisfaction, no question. But ultimately you will wind up disappointed and disillusioned.

Since I am committed to what is best for you, I am not going to suggest, "Oh, well, do whatever." I am going to challenge you to keep an eternal perspective, even though you are in the minority.

Go God's way! His is the most reliable route to follow when life gets complicated. It will have its tough moments, but you will never regret it.

Your attitude is a choice you make each day.

*Acknowledgments*

⁓

Grateful acknowledgment is made to the
following publishers for permission to reprint
this copyrighted material. All copyrights are
held by the author, Charles R. Swindoll.

*Living Above the Level of Mediocrity* (Nashville: W Publishing
Group, 1981).

*Strengthening Your Grip* (Nashville: W Publishing Group,
1982).

*Living on the Ragged Edge* (Nashville: W Publishing Group,
1985).

*Living Beyond the Daily Grind* (Nashville: W Publishing
Group, 1988).

*The Grace Awakening* (Nashville: W Publishing Group, 1990).

*Simple Faith* (Nashville: W Publishing Group, 1993).

*The Finishing Touch* (Nashville: W Publishing Group, 1994).

*Laugh Again* (Nashville: W Publishing Group, 1994).

*Hope Again* (Nashville: W Publishing Group, 1996).

*Three Steps Forward, Two Steps Back*, revised edition
(Nashville: W Publishing Group, 1997)

*David: A Man of Passion and Destiny* (Nashville:
W Publishing Group, 1997).

*Swindoll's Ultimate Book of Illustrations & Quotes* (Nashville:
W Publishing Group, 1998).

*Joseph: A Man of Integrity and Forgiveness* (Nashville:
W Publishing Group, 1998).

*The Mystery of God's Will* (Nashville: W Publishing Group,
1999).

*Esther: A Woman of Strength and Dignity* (Nashville:
W Publishing Group, 1999).

*Moses: A Man of Selfless Dedication* (Nashville: W Publishing
Group, 1999).

*Day by Day with Charles Swindoll* (Nashville: W Publishing
Group, 2000).

*Paul: A Man of Grace and Grit* (Nashville: W Publishing,
2002)

*Job: A Man of Heroic Endurance* (Nashville: W Publishing,
2004)

*Getting Through the Tough Stuff* (Nashville: W Publishing,
2004)

*So, You Want to Be Like Christ?* (Nashville: W Publishing,
2005)

*"Taking on Life with a Great Attitude,"* sermon by Charles R.
Swindoll